J Bio Judge

y

Baseball Superstar Aaron Judge

by Jon M. Fishman

LERNER PUBLICATIONS ◆ MINNEAPOLIS

Note to Educators

Throughout this book, you'll find critical-thinking questions. These can be used to engage young readers in thinking critically about the topic and in using the text and photos to do so.

Lerner Publications Company
A division of Lerner Publishing Group, Inc.
241 First Avenue North
Minneapolis, MN 55401 USA

For reading levels and more information, look up this title at www.lernerbooks.com.

Library of Congress Cataloging-in-Publication Data

Names: Fishman, Jon M., author.
Title: Baseball superstar Aaron Judge / by Jon M. Fishman.
Description: Minneapolis, Minnesota : Lerner Publications, [2019] | Series: Bumba Books — Sports Superstars | Audience: Ages: 4–7. | Audience: Grades: K to Grade 3. | Includes bibliographical references and index.
Identifiers: LCCN 2018019334 (print) | LCCN 2018024704 (ebook) | ISBN 9781541542976 (eb pdf) | ISBN 9781541538511 (library binding : alk. paper) | ISBN 9781541545755 (paperback : alk. paper)
Subjects: LCSH: Judge, Aaron, 1992– —Juvenile literature. | Baseball players—United States—Biography—Juvenile literature.
Classification: LCC GV865.J83 (ebook) | LCC GV865.J83 F573 2019 (print) | DDC 796.357092 [B]—dc23

LC record available at https://lccn.loc.gov/2018019334

Manufactured in the United States of America
1-45034-35861-7/11/2018

Table of
Contents

Big Hitter

Aaron Judge plays baseball for the

New York Yankees.

He is a superstar outfielder.

Aaron was taller than most kids his age.

He hit the baseball farther than other kids too.

Baseball was Aaron's favorite sport. He also played football and basketball.

Why do people play sports?

Aaron went to college in California.

He played college baseball for

three years.

11

He joined the New York Yankees after college.

Aaron became one of the team's best players.

What are some ways to be a good teammate?

13

Aaron hit 52 home runs in 2017.

It was a great season.

He won the 2017 Home Run Derby.

He hit lots of home runs.

Aaron is one of the biggest players in baseball.

He works hard to keep his body strong.

Aaron is just getting started.

He plans to hit many more home runs!

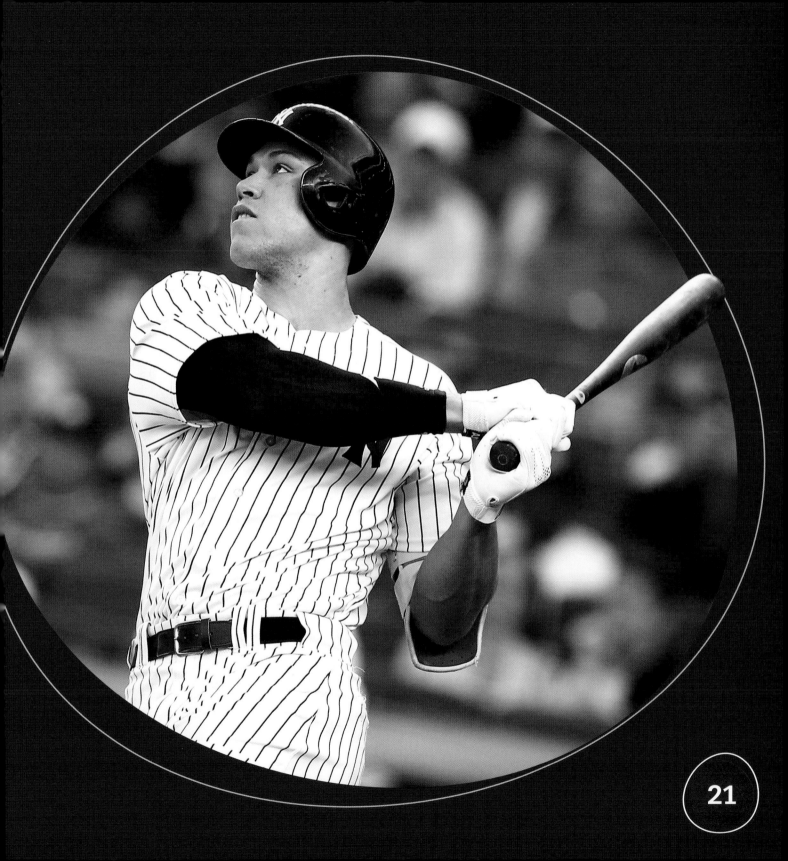

Baseball Gear

baseball

bat

glove

helmet

Picture Glossary

college

school after high school

Home Run Derby

a contest to see who can hit the most home runs

home runs

hits that let the batter run to home plate to score

outfielder

a player who plays in the grass beyond the infield

23

Read More

Derr, Aaron. *Baseball: An Introduction to Being a Good Sport.* Egremont, MA: Red Chair, 2017.

Flynn, Brendan. *Baseball Time!* Minneapolis: Lerner Publications, 2017.

Schuh, Mari. *Baseball.* Mankato, MN: Amicus, 2018.

Index

Photo Credits

Image credits: Amy Salveson/Independent Picture Service (baseball icons throughout); Paul Bereswill/Getty Images, pp. 5, 13, 18, 23 (bottom right); Bob Levey/Getty Images, p. 6; Cliff Welch/Icon Sports Wire/Getty Images, pp. 8–9; Josh Holmberg/Cal Sport Media/AP Images, pp. 10, 23 (top left); Billie Weiss/Boston Red Sox/Getty Images, pp. 14–15, 23 (bottom left); Brace Hemmelgarn/Minnesota Twins/Getty Images, pp. 17, 23 (top right); Mike Stobe/Getty Images, p. 21; Todd Strand/Independent Picture Service, p. 22 (baseball); CrackerClips Stock Media/Shutterstock.com, p. 22 (bat); Bobby Stevens Photo/Shutterstock.com, p. 22 (helmet); GMessina/Shutterstock.com, p. 22 (glove).

Cover: Paul Bereswill/Getty Images.